PIANO SOLOS

Sacred Christmas

M000105128

Arranged by: Shannon M. Grama

ISBN 0-7935-3311-2

HAL•LEONARD
CORPORATION

7777 W. BLUEMOUND RD. P.O. BOX 13819 MILWAUKEE, WI 53213

ANGELS FROM THE REALMS OF GLORY

Words by JAMES MONTGOMERY
Music by HENRY SMART

ANGELS WE HAVE HEARD ON HIGH

AVE MARIA/SILENT NIGHT

AVE MARIA
By FRANZ SCHUBERT

SILENT NIGHT
Words by JOSEPH MOHR
Music by FRANZ GRUBER

Gently flowing

AWAY IN A MANGER

Words by MARTIN LUTHER
Music by JONATHAN E. SPILLMAN

THE FIRST NOEL

rall.

a tempo

mp

hold pedal down throughout this section

8va -
sim.

chime-like, without variation in dynamics

- loco

GO TELL IT ON THE MOUNTAIN

HARK! THE HERALD ANGELS SING

Words by CHARLES WESLEY
Music by FELIX MENDELSSOHN-BARTHOLDY

With pomp and fanfare

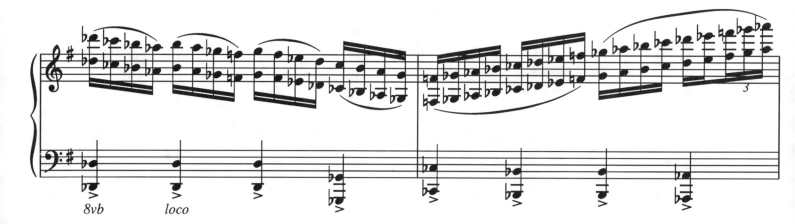

IT CAME UPON THE MIDNIGHT CLEAR

Words by EDMUND H. SEARS
Music by RICHARD S. WILLIS

O HOLY NIGHT

English Words by D.S. DWIGHT
Music by ADOLPHE ADAM

8va lower⌐

JOY TO THE WORLD

Words by ISAAC WATTS
Music by GEORGE F. HANDEL

L'istesso tempo

OH COME, ALL YE FAITHFUL
(Adeste Fidelis)

Latin words translated by FREDERICK OAKELEY
Music by JOHN READING

42

O COME, O COME EMMANUEL

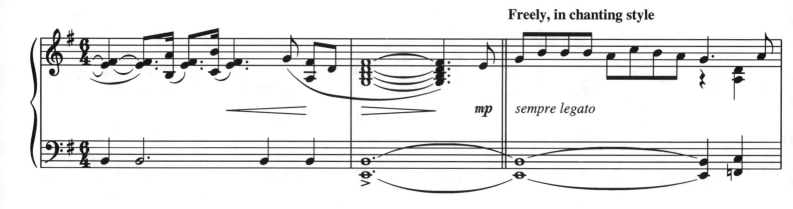

ONCE IN ROYAL DAVID'S CITY

Words by C.F. ALEXANDER
Music by H.J. GAUNTLETT

Calmly

WHAT CHILD IS THIS?

Very freely

O LITTLE TOWN OF BETHLEHEM

Words by PHILLIPS BROOKS
Music by LEWIS H. REDNER

Serenely

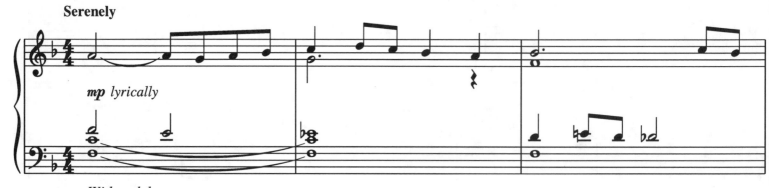